Conversation Starters

for

Markus Zusak's

The Book Thief

By dailyBooks

  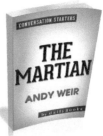

Tips for Using dailyBooks Conversation Starters:

EVERY GOOD BOOK CONTAINS A WORLD FAR DEEPER THAN the surface of its pages. The characters and their world come alive through the words on the pages, yet the characters and its world still live on. Questions herein are designed to bring us beneath the surface of the page and invite us into the world that lives on. These questions can be used to:

- Foster a deeper understanding of the book
- Promote an atmosphere of discussion for groups
- Assist in the study of the book, either individually or corporately
- Explore unseen realms of the book as never seen before

About Us:

THROUGH YEARS OF EXPERIENCE AND FIELD EXPERTISE, from newspaper featured book clubs to local library chapters, *dailyBooks* can bring your book discussion to life. Host your book party as we discuss some of today's most widely read books.

Table of Contents

Introducing *The Book Thief*

THE BOOK THIEF TELLS THE STORY OF LIESEL FROM Germany during World War II. Liesel and her brother were placed in foster care by their mother, and her brother suddenly dies. Liesel is traumatized by this and suffers greatly with nightmares when she sleeps as a result.

To help with her nightmares, Liesel's foster father, Hans, teaches her to read when she wakes up with nightmares. He hopes that learning to read will distract her from the trauma and nightmares. Eventually, books become Liesel'scomfort, and her school performance improves. During the war, Liesel begins to steal books in order to feel comfort in the chaos and cruelty surrounding her.

Liesel also helps her foster mother, Rosa, do laundry to earn some money. When the war starts, Liesel is responsible for doing the laundry herself. Rosa believes that the customers will not fire a child; however, she soon discovers that is not the case. The last laundry customer is the mayor's wife, Ilsa. One night, Ilsa discovers Liesel pulling a book out of a Nazi fire. Liesel fears that she will be arrested if Ilsa tells someone, but rather Ilsa allows Lieselaccess to her personal library. Liesel spends much of her time in the library until Ilsa breaks the news that she must fire Rosa. Ilsa tries to give Liesel *The Whistler*, but Liesel refuses.

Liesel has also been stealing food with her friend Rudy, which gives her confidence to steal other things. She decides to go into Ilsa's library and steal *The Whistler*. When she finishes the book, she returns it and takes another. Ilsa eventually finds out what Liesel is doing and starts leaving her presents.

Liesel's foster parents also hide a Jewish man, Max, in their house. Hans makes Liesel promise she will not tell anyone about Max. Liesel and Max both have nightmares, which allows them to bond with one another. One day, Hans sees an elderly Jewish man being marched through the city. Hans gives him a piece of bread but is caught and beaten by the Gestapo. Hans is afraid for his life and sends Max away. Hans is then forced to join the Nazi party. He returns home with a broken leg.

One night, a bomb is mistakenly dropped on the house. Liesel survives because she is in the basement writing her story, but Hans, Rosa, and Rudy all die. Liesel kisses Rudy when she discovers that he is dead. Liesel is then taken in by Ilsa. She is eventually reunited with Max, who tells her how he lived in the Dachau concentration camp. The story ends with Liesel's death, and Death tells how she lived a long and happy life with her husband and children.

Introducing the Author

MARKUS ZUSAK WAS BORN IN SYNDEY IN THE YEAR 1975. Zusak was born to European immigrants. His father, Helmut, was originally from Austria, and his mother, Lisa, was originally from Germany. Zusak grew up with an older brother and two older sisters.

After high school, Zusak attended university, where he was a student of History and English. Following his graduation, he returned to his childhood high school and taught English.

Zusak's first book, *The Underdog*, was published in 1999. His following two bookswere released in 2000 and 2001, respectively. All three books reached international recognition and received numerous literary awards.

Zusak'snext book, *The Messenger*, was published in 2002 and, like his others, reached international recognition. The book was called *I Am the Messenger* in the United States where it was nominated for the Printz Award.

In 2005, Zusak's well-known and most popular novel, *The Book Thief*, was published. Zusak stated that he used parts of his mother's story growing up in Germany as a child to write the story. The book was published in over thirty languages and remained at the top of the *New York Times* and Amazon.com bestseller list for several weeks. It was also number one in Taiwan, Brazil, and Ireland. It also won the Kathleen Mitchell Award in 2006.andin 2013, the bookwas adapted into a film.

Zusak was the recipient of the Margaret A. Edwards Award, in 2014, which is given by the American Library Association for significant contribution to literature.

Discussion Questions

question 1

Two of the themes in *The Book Thief* are human cruelty and self-sacrifice. What are some examples of human cruelty and self-sacrifice throughout the story?

. . . .

question 2

Guilt is another theme in *The Book Thief*. What are some examples of guilt
throughout the story?

. . . .

question 3

Liesel and Max have similar stories in *The Book Thief.* What are some ways that Liesel and Max are similar? What are some ways that they are different?

question 4

Liesel and Max are both staying with Hans and Rosa during the war. At what point in the story did they become friends? Why do you think they became friends?

. . . .

question 5

Liesel finds comfort in reading books. What are some examples in the story of times Liesel felt comforted by reading?

. . . .

question 6

Ilsa ends up taking in Liesel after Hans and Rosa die. How does the relationship between Ilsa and Liesel change over time? Compare and contrast the beginning of their relationship to their relationship at the end of the novel. Why do you think their relationship changed?

. . . .

question 7

A theme in *The Book Thief* is courage. Give some examples of how Liesel, Hans, Rosa, Rudy, Max, and Ilsa show courage in the novel? Why do you think they were able to be so courageous during the war?

. . . .

question 8

Liesel loses nearly everyone in her life in some way. How did she handle each of these losses? What did she do to find comfort and courage despite these great losses?

. . . .

. . . .

question 9

At the end of the book, Death carries Liesel's book with him wherever he goes. Why do you think Death chose to do this?

. . . .

. . . .

question 10

Liesel steals many books throughout *The Book Thief*. Why do you think she stole so many books? Are the book titles she steals significant in any way? Why or why not?

. . . .

question 11

Liesel is described as a "girl with a mountain to climb." What do you think the mountain is that she must climb? Is anyone climbing the metaphorical mountain with her or helping her along the way?

．　．

question 12

The ending of *The Book Thief* does not mention who Liesel married. Who do you think Liesel married? Why do you think this? What evidence is there to support your opinion?

．　．

question 13

At the end of the book, Death says, "I'm haunted by humans." What do you think this quote means? What evidence is there to support your opinion?

. . . .

question 14

Liesel endures many hardships through the story. She also encounters many people. What do you think is the moral of this story, if any? Why do you think as you do?

. . . .

question 15

Liesel does not tell Rudy that Max is hiding in the basement. Do you think that she could have trusted Rudy with that secret? Why or why not?

question 16

A few readers found that it was difficult to feel interested in the story at the beginning of *The Book Thief*. However, after the beginning, they found the book to be more interesting. Do you agree with these readers? Why or why not?

. . . .

question 17

Some readers enjoy Death as a narrator and others do not like that the story is
narrated by Death. How do you feel about Death as a narrator? Why do you
feel as you do?

. . . .

question 18

The Book Thief has been added to the list of banned books in schools. Why do you think this book is banned? Do you agree that this book should be banned? Why or why not?

. . . .

question 19

One reader commented that *The Book Thief* stands out because it is about a German orphan during World War II. Other Holocaust books tend to focus on Jews in concentration camps. Do you agree with this reader? Do you think this book is unique in comparison to other books about the Holocaust? Why or why not?

. . . .

question 20

One reader felt as though Markus Zusak did not do enough research on World War II or The Holocaust. Therefore, he did not write an accurate historical fiction book with *The Book Thief*. Do you agree with this reader? Why or why not?

 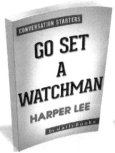 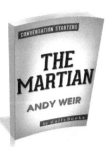

question 21

One reader did not like that Death tells the reader that something bad will happen before it happens. They felt as though it spoiled the surprise, thus, it was not as emotional for them as it could have been. Do you agree with this reader? Why or why not?

. . . .

. . . .

question 22

Some readers like the descriptive wording Markus Zusak uses in this story. Other readers strongly dislike it. What are your thoughts on the descriptive phrases Zusak uses? Do you like how the book was written? Why or why not?

. . . .

. . . .

question 23

The Book Thief remained at the top of numerous bestseller lists for several weeks. Why do you believe this book was so popular? Do you think it is deserving of the recognition it has received? Why or why not?

. . . .

question 24

One reader stated that *The Book Thief* was an "ode to those who kept their humanity in the middle of war." The reader then went on to list characters like Rudy, Hans, Rosa, and Max as examples of this description. Do you agree with this reader? Why or why not?

. . . .

question 25

A few readers have mentioned that they enjoyed the characters, writing, and uniqueness of *The Book Thief*. However, they did not enjoy the story line. Do you agree with these readers? Why or why not?

. . . .

. . . .

question 26

To write his fourth book, *The Book Thief*, Markus Zusak included parts of his mother's experiences growing up in Germany during World War II. Do you think this personal account of the period is helpful to an author? Do you think the author should do more research when writing historical fiction? Why or why not?

. . . .

. . . .

question 27

Markus Zusak earned an English and History degree in college. Do you think his education helped him when writing his novels? Why or why not?

. . . .

. . . .

question 28

Markus Zusak has twice been a runner-up for the Printz Award. Why do you
think he has yet to win the award? Do you think it is possible for him to win
the award? Why or why not?

. . . .

. . . .

question 29

Markus Zusak worked as an English teacher before becoming a full-time novelist. Do you think his job as an English teacher helped him at all when writing novels? Why or why not?

. . . .

. . . .

question 30

His book, *The Messenger*, was retitled to *I Am the Messenger* in the United States. Why do you think Zusak or his publishers decided to change the title of the novel? Do you agree with the change? Why or why not?

. . . .

. . . .

question 31

The Book Thief is told from the perspective of Death. How would the story be different if it were told from Liesel's perspective? How would it be different if it were told from Max's or Hans's perspective?

. . . .

question 32

Liesel suffers many great losses in her life. Would you have dealt with those losses in the same way Liesel does? Why or why not?

. . . .

question 33

Hans keeps Max, a Jewish man, hidden in his house during the war. If you were Hans, would you have done the same thing? Would you have hidden someone in your house knowing the risks to you and your family? Why or why not?

. . . .

. . . .

question 34

Liesel must keep a family secret in the novel. If you were Liesel, would you be able to keep the secret? Would you tell someone? How do you think your family would react to the secret?

. . . .

. . . .

question 35

In the book, Liesel and Rudy are close friends. Liesel refuses to kiss Rudy. When she finds that Rudy has died, she finally kisses him. Do you think if Rudy had lived that Liesel would have married him at the end of the story? Why or why not?

. . . .

question 36

At the beginning of *The Book Thief*, Liesel's brother dies. Do you think the story would have been different had her brother lived? What effect do you think his presence would have had on the story?

. . . .

question 37

At the beginning of the novel, Liesel and her brother are being placed with foster parents. If you were Liesel, how would you have felt to leave your parents and home to live with strange people during a war? Would you have felt the same as Liesel? Why or why not?

. . . .

question 38

After Hans and Rosa die, Liesel goes to live with Ilsa. If Liesel had not met Ilsa nor become her friend, where do you think Liesel would have gone to live?

Quiz Questions

. . . .

question39

The main character of the story is _____. In the
beginning of the novel, she goes to live with foster parents.

. . . .

question40

Liesel is living with _____ during World War II. It is there she discovers her love of reading and writing.

question41

Hans and Rosa are a German family who does not agree with Hitler's way of living. They secretly allow _____, a Jewish man, to live with them during World War II.

. . . .

question42

In the story, Liesel has a best friend named _____. He is described as having hair the color of lemons. He and Liesel steal food together.

. . . .

question 43

Liesel works with her foster mother, Rosa, doing laundry. One day, Liesel meets the mayor's wife, Ilsa. Ilsa allows Liesel to use her _____.

question 44

True or False: The title, *The Book Thief*, is speaking of Liesel, since she often steals books throughout the novel.

. . . .

question 45

True or False: A bomb hits the Hubermann house killing Hans, Rosa, and Rudy. Liesel survives the bomb because she stays in the basement writing her story.

. . . .

question 46

The author of *The Book Thief* is _____. He was born in Australia in 1975.

. . . .

question 47

The author is the son of two European immigrants. His father was from
Austria, and his mother was from _____.

. . . .

question 48

After high school, the author studied
_____ in college.

question 49

True or False: The author's latest book, *The Book Thief*, has been published in over thirty languages.

question 50

True or False: The author's first book was called *I Am the Messenger.*

QuizAnswers

1. Liesel (Meminger)
2. Hans and Rosa (Hubermann)
3. Max (Vandenburg)
4. Rudy
5. library
6. True
7. True
8. Markus Zusak
9. Germany
10. English and History
11. True
12. False; His first book was *The Underdog*.

THE END

Want to promote your book group?
Register here.

  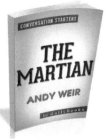

Made in United States
Troutdale, OR
07/26/2023

11562957R00040